VEGETARIAN
FOR ONE

© 1999 Rebo International b.v., Lisse, The Netherlands
1999 Published by Rebo Productions Ltd., London
Designed and created by Consortium, England

Recipes and photographs on pages 16–17, 18–19,
22–23, 24–25, 28–29, 30–31, 32–33, 36–37,
40–41, 50–51, 52–53, 60–61, 68–69,
76–77, 80–81, 82–83, 86–87, 90–91, 94–95
© Ceres Verlag, Rudolf-August Oetker KG, Bielefeld, Germany
All other recipes and photographs © Quadrillion
Publishing Ltd, Godalming, Surrey GU7 1XW

Typeset by MATS, Southend-on-Sea, Essex
Printed in Slovenia

Ceres Verlag recipes compiled and translated by
Stephen Challacombe
Edited by Anne Sheasby
Illustrations by Camilla Sopwith
Cover design by Minkowsky, Enkhuizen,
The Netherlands

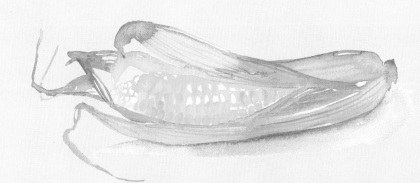

VEGETARIAN
FOR ONE

EASY YET EXCITING DISHES FOR EVERYDAY EATING

REBO PRODUCTIONS

Contents

Introduction

Whether you're a full-time vegetarian or someone who likes to eat vegetarian food for part of the week or occasionally, you may have found it hard to find recipes geared to your particular needs and desires when cooking just for yourself. Getting the right balance between vegetarian dishes that excite the eye and the tastebuds while being relatively quick and easy to prepare can present quite a challenge – especially when you would rather avoid having to revisit the same food the next day!

At the same time, cooking for oneself offers the opportunity to explore and delight in whatever fresh and exotic ingredients take your fancy from the wealth now freely available to the vegetarian. Besides luscious fruits, tender vegetables and aromatic herbs of all kinds, there are peppery salad leaves, fragrant grains, flavoured pastas and nutty pulses to enjoy, not forgetting mellow vegetarian cheeses and wonderfully savoury smoked tofu.

In this book, we present a collection of varied vegetarian recipes specially selected for cooking for one. They are light on your time and culinary skills yet heavy on flavour interest, exploiting to great effect many of those quality ingredients we've just mentioned. Liven up your lunchtime with colourful kebabs, a crunchy vegetable salad or a creamy chilled soup. Spice up your suppertime with a vegetarian chilli, bean curry or a piquant pasta dish. And add to your delectable meal a fitting finale in the form of a wickedly rich and sumptuous or cool and refreshing dessert, according to your mood and appetite. Whichever recipe you choose, you'll be glad that it's all just for you!

Pamplemousse

A refreshing mixed fruit starter which is simple and quick to prepare.

Preparation time: 10 minutes • Serves: 1

Ingredients

½ grapefruit (cut in half crossways)	4 grapes (black or green)
1 small red skinned apple	15 ml (1 tbsp) double cream
1 stick celery	

Method

1

Cut around the inside of the skin of the grapefruit half to loosen the flesh.

2

Make deep cuts between the segments close to the membranes and remove the segments,
making sure you do not pierce the skin.

3

Place the segments in a bowl with any of the juice.

4

Cut away and discard any remaining membranes from the grapefruit shell with a pair of kitchen scissors,
place the shell in a plastic bag and store in the refrigerator until required.

5

Remove the core from the apple and dice but do not peel.

6

Finely chop the celery.

7

Halve the grapes and remove the seeds, if necessary.

8

Add the apple, celery and grapes to the grapefruit segments and stir in the double cream. Refrigerate until required.

9

Just before serving, stir well and pile the mixture into the grapefruit shell. Serve at once.

Serving suggestion

To make Vandyke grapefruit, snip small V-shapes from the edges of the empty half shell. Serve garnished with fresh mint leaves.

Variations

Use pink, white or ruby grapefruit for this recipe. Use a pear in place of the apple.
Use crème fraîche or Greek yogurt in place of cream.

Savoury Tomato

This light yet delicious dish is an ideal low-fat and calorie appetiser.

Preparation time: 10 minutes • Serves: 1

Ingredients

1 large Spanish tomato	*Salt and freshly ground black pepper*
15 ml (1 tbsp) cottage cheese	*15 g (½ oz) pumpkin seeds*
1.25 ml (¼ tsp) ground cumin	*Watercress sprigs, to serve*
½ green pepper, seeded and diced	

Method

1
Slice off the top of the tomato.

2
Remove and discard the seeds and leave the tomato upside down to drain.

3
Rub the cottage cheese through a sieve to achieve a smooth consistency – add a little milk if necessary.

4
Stir in the cumin, green pepper and salt and pepper to taste.

5
Fill the tomato with the cheese mixture.

6
Dry roast the pumpkin seeds in a frying pan until lightly browned. Sprinkle over the tomato. Chill until required.

7
Serve on a bed of watercress sprigs.

Serving suggestions
Serve with thin slices of lightly buttered brown bread or crispbreads.

Variations
Use cream cheese in place of the cottage cheese. Use ground coriander in place of cumin.
Use sunflower or sesame seeds in place of pumpkin seeds.

Carrot and Sweetcorn Medley

This delectable combination is flavoured with garlic, lemon juice and fresh ginger.

Preparation time: 10 minutes, plus chilling time • Serves: 1

Ingredients

115 g (4 oz) carrots	*85 g (3 oz) canned sweetcorn, drained*
½ clove garlic, crushed	*Finely shredded lettuce, to serve*
15 ml (1 tbsp) lemon juice	*1.25 ml (¼ tsp) grated fresh root ginger*
Salt and freshly ground black pepper	*1-2 black olives, stoned*

Method

1
Scrub and grate the carrots and place in a bowl.

2
Place the garlic, lemon juice and salt and pepper in a small screw-topped jar and shake well to mix.

3
Pour the dressing over the grated carrot, add the sweetcorn and toss to mix.

4
Place a little lettuce in the bottom of an individual stemmed glass and arrange the carrot and sweetcorn mixture over the top.

5
Garnish with the grated ginger and olives.

6
Chill for 30 minutes before serving.

Serving suggestion
Serve with wholemeal bread and butter triangles.

Variations
Use raw beetroot or mooli in place of carrot. Use canned (rinsed and drained) flageolet or black-eyed beans
in place of sweetcorn. Use lime juice in place of lemon juice.

Cook's tip
To use as an accompaniment to a main course, arrange the carrot on a serving plate,
leave an indentation in the centre and fill this with the sweetcorn. Garnish with ginger and olives.

Fennel and Orange Croustade

Fragrant fennel and tangy orange combine perfectly to make an exciting topping for crisp, deep-fried bread.

Preparation time: 15 minutes • Cooking time: 5 minutes • Serves: 1

Ingredients

2.5-cm (1-in) thick slice wholemeal bread	*1 orange*
Oil, for deep frying	*5 ml (1 tsp) olive oil*
½ fennel bulb	*A pinch of salt*
(reserve any fronds for garnishing)	*A fresh mint sprig, to garnish*

Method

1
Trim and discard the crusts from the bread, then cut into a 7.5-cm (3-in) square.

2
Hollow out the middle of the bread leaving an evenly shaped case.

3
Heat the oil in a pan or deep-fat fryer and deep-fry the bread until golden brown. Carefully remove the bread from the hot oil.

4
Drain the bread thoroughly on absorbent kitchen paper. Leave to cool.

5
Trim the fennel, reserving the fronds, then thinly slice. Place in a bowl.

6
Remove all the peel and pith from the orange and cut into segments – do this over the bowl containing the fennel to catch the juice.

7
Mix the orange segments with the fennel.

8
Add the olive oil and salt and mix together thoroughly.

9
Just before serving, pile the fennel and orange mixture into the bread case and garnish with a fresh mint sprig and fennel fronds. Serve.

Serving suggestions
Serve with a mixed leaf salad or crunchy coleslaw.

Variations
Use white or granary bread in place of wholemeal bread. Use ½ pink grapefruit in place of the orange.
Use walnut or hazelnut oil in place of olive oil.

Cook's tip
The salad can be made in advance and refrigerated until required but do not fill the bread case until just before serving.

Cold Tomato Soup with Avocado Cream

A delicious fresh tomato soup – ideal for a summertime treat alfresco.

Preparation time: 20 minutes • Serves: 1

Ingredients

250 g (9 oz) ripe tomatoes	½ clove garlic, crushed
1 shallot, finely chopped	30 ml (2 tbsp) milk
20 ml (4 tsp) olive oil	10 ml (2 tsp) lemon juice
10 ml (2 tsp) wine vinegar	Sugar, to taste
Salt and freshly ground black pepper	A fresh mint sprig, to garnish
½ small avocado pear	

Method

1

Chop the tomatoes, then purée in a food processor or blender until smooth. Press through a sieve and reserve the pulp, discarding the skin and seeds. Place the tomato pulp in a bowl.

2

Stir the shallot, oil and wine vinegar into the tomato pulp and mix well. Season to taste with salt and pepper and set aside.

3

For the avocado cream, peel and stone the avocado, then slice the flesh.

4

Place the sliced avocado in a bowl, then mix with the garlic, milk, lemon juice, sugar and salt to taste.

5

Blend the avocado mixture in a food processor or blender until smooth and well mixed.

6

Serve the tomato soup in a soup bowl and spoon the avocado cream into the centre of the soup.

7

Serve, garnished with a fresh mint sprig.

Serving suggestions

Serve with fresh crusty bread or toast.

Variations

Use plum tomatoes in place of standard tomatoes. Use crème fraîche in place of milk.

Vegetable Soup with Shoots

A nutritious soup for a satisfying supper or lunch.

Preparation time: 10 minutes • Cooking time: 20 minutes • Serves: 1

Ingredients

5 ml (1 tsp) olive oil	*200 ml (7 fl oz) vegetable stock*
½ clove garlic, crushed	*2.5 ml (½ tsp) paprika*
½ red pepper, seeded and sliced	*1 handful vegetable shoots, such as alfalfa or cress*
30-45 ml (2-3 tbsp) canned haricot beans, drained	*A fresh herb sprig, to garnish*

Method

1

Heat the oil in a saucepan and add the garlic. Cook briefly, stirring.

2

Add the pepper and cook for 4-5 minutes, stirring occasionally.

3

Add the beans and stock to the pan with the paprika and mix well.

4

Bring to the boil, cover and cook gently for 10 minutes, stirring occasionally.

5

Add the vegetable shoots to the pan and stir. Allow to cook very briefly, then adjust the seasoning.

6

Serve the soup immediately in a warmed soup bowl, garnished with a fresh herb sprig.

Serving suggestion

Serve with a wholemeal or granary roll.

Variations

Use canned red kidney beans or chick-peas in place of haricot beans. Use yellow or green pepper in place of red.
Use a little grated fresh root ginger in place of garlic.

Sweet Potato Soup

Warm up your winter nights with this heartening soup.

Preparation time: 10 minutes • Cooking time: 45-60 minutes • Serves: 1

Ingredients

15 g (½ oz) butter or margarine	*A little lemon rind and juice*
½ small onion, finely chopped	*200 ml (7 fl oz) vegetable stock*
115 g (4 oz) sweet potato, diced	*Freshly ground black pepper*
55 g (2 oz) carrots, diced	*A fresh coriander leaf, to garnish*
5 ml (1 tsp) chopped fresh coriander	

Method

1

Melt the butter or margarine in a pan and cook the onion until transparent, stirring occasionally.

2

Add the sweet potato and carrots and allow to 'sweat' over a very low heat for 10-15 minutes, stirring occasionally.

3

Add the chopped coriander, lemon rind and juice, stock and pepper.

4

Cover and simmer for 30-40 minutes, stirring occasionally.

5

Cool slightly, then liquidise until almost smooth but leaving some texture to the soup.

6

Return to the rinsed-out pan and reheat until piping hot, stirring occasionally.

7

Garnish with a fresh coriander leaf and serve immediately.

Serving suggestion

Serve with a granary roll or bap.

Variations

Use fresh parsley or basil in place of coriander. Use standard potatoes in place of sweet potatoes,
Use a small leek in place of the onion. Use parsnips in place of carrots.

Cook's tip

Fresh coriander can be kept in a jug of water in a cool place. It can also be frozen for use when fresh is not available.

Soups

Carrot and Rice Soup with Lemon

An unusual, piquant soup for a starter or light lunch.

Preparation time: 10 minutes • Cooking time: 30-35 minutes • Serves: 1

Ingredients

15 ml (1 tbsp) butter	*1 small carrot, thinly sliced*
1 shallot, thinly sliced	*Juice of ½ small lemon*
25 g (1 oz) long-grain rice	*15 ml (1 tbsp) crème fraîche*
300 ml (½ pint) vegetable stock	*Lemon slices, to garnish*
Salt and grated nutmeg, to taste	

Method

1

Heat the butter in a pan, add the shallot and cook for 5 minutes, until softened, stirring occasionally.

2

Add the rice to the pan, stir well, then cook briefly, stirring continuously, before adding the stock.

3

Bring to the boil, cover and simmer for about 20 minutes, until the rice is almost cooked and tender, stirring occasionally.

4

Season with salt and grated nutmeg.

5

Add the sliced carrot to the soup and cook for a further 5 minutes.

6

Stir in the lemon juice and crème fraîche and cook briefly until hot, stirring.

7

Serve immediately, garnished with lemon slices.

Serving suggestions

Serve with crusty French bread or pitta bread.

Variations

Use a parsnip or courgette in place of the carrot. Use double cream in place of crème fraîche.

Chilled Tomato and Apricot Soup

An appetising soup, full of refreshing flavour.

Preparation time: 20 minutes, plus cooling and chilling times • Cooking time: 10 minutes • Serves: 1

Ingredients

15 g (½ oz) butter	A pinch of sugar
1 shallot, thinly sliced	225-g (8-oz) can apricots in fruit juice
225-g (8-oz) can peeled tomatoes	30 ml (1 fl oz) dry white wine
Chopped fresh oregano or marjoram, to taste	50 ml (2 fl oz) single cream
Salt and freshly ground black pepper	A fresh herb sprig and croutons, to garnish

Method

1
Melt the butter in a pan, then add the shallot, tomatoes, oregano or marjoram and salt and pepper to taste.

2
Cook gently for 10 minutes, stirring occasionally. Adjust the seasoning to make a piquant flavour, then add the sugar.

3
Purée the mixture in a food processor or blender until smooth. Set aside to cool.

4
Purée the apricots with the wine, 15 ml (1 tbsp) water and cream in a food processor or blender until smooth.

5
Pass the mixture through a sieve, discarding any pulp remaining in the sieve.

6
Return the apricot mixture to the food processor or blender together with the cooled tomato mixture.

7
Blend until thoroughly mixed, then pour into a bowl and chill before serving.

8
Serve, garnished with the fresh herb sprig and croutons.

Serving suggestion
Serve with thin slices of wholemeal bread.

Variations
Use pears or peaches in place of apricots. Use unsweetened fruit juice such as apple or orange in place of wine.

Cook's tip
Instead of blending the tomato mixture and apricot purée together, chill separately, then swirl together in a serving bowl.

Nutty Potato Cakes

This is the perfect way to use up leftover potatoes, to create a tasty snack.

Preparation time: 10 minutes • Cooking time: 25 minutes • Serves: 1

Ingredients

115 g (4 oz) potatoes	*1 spring onion, finely chopped*
A knob of butter	*Freshly ground black pepper*
A little milk	*Wholemeal flour, for coating*
15 g (½ oz) mixed nuts, finely ground	*Vegetable oil, for frying*
10 g (¼ oz) sunflower seeds, finely ground	

Method

1
Peel the potatoes and cut into pieces. Cook in a pan of boiling water until just soft.

2
Drain and mash the potatoes with butter and milk to a creamy consistency.

3
Add the nuts, seeds, spring onion and pepper to taste, mixing well.

4
If necessary, add a little more milk at this stage to give a soft texture which holds together.

5
Form the mixture into 2 round cakes.

6
Coat with flour and fry quickly in a frying pan in a little oil until golden brown on both sides.

7
Drain on absorbent kitchen paper and serve hot.

Serving suggestion
Serve with a green salad and sliced tomatoes in an oil and fresh basil dressing.

Variations
Dry-roast the sunflower seeds until golden brown before grinding, if you like. Use sweet potatoes in place of standard potatoes. Use pumpkin or sesame seeds in place of sunflower seeds.

Mixed Vegetables with Lemon Butter

Lightly cooked vegetables are served in a creamy, tangy sauce.

Preparation time: 15 minutes • Cooking time: 10 minutes • Serves: 1

Ingredients

250 g (9 oz) mixed vegetables such as carrots, sugar-snap peas, kohlrabi and celeriac	Rind of ½ lemon
	Salt and freshly ground black pepper
30 ml (2 tbsp) butter	30-45 ml (2-3 tbsp) double cream
5 ml (1 tsp) lemon juice	15 ml (1 tbsp) chopped fresh chervil or chives

Method

1
Peel or trim the vegetables, then cut into small pieces.

2
Place the prepared vegetables in a shallow pan, add a little water and cover. Cook for about 10 minutes, until cooked and tender, stirring occasionally.

3
Meanwhile, melt the butter in a pan, add the lemon juice and rind and salt and pepper to taste, then pour on the cream. Beat vigorously.

4
Drain and serve the vegetables on a warm plate, sprinkle with the chopped herbs and pour the sauce over the top. Serve immediately.

Serving suggestions
Serve with garlic or herb-flavoured bread or boiled rice.

Variations
Choose your own selection of mixed vegetables. Use lime or orange rind and juice in place of lemon. Use crème fraîche in place of cream.

Greek-Style Vegetable Kebabs

These appetising kebabs combine vegetarian sheep's cheese with a mixture of Mediterranean vegetables.

Preparation time: 25 minutes, plus 10 minutes marinating time • Cooking time: 15 minutes • Serves: 1

Ingredients

4 cherry tomatoes	*30 ml (2 tbsp) olive oil*
Salt and freshly ground black pepper	*Dried oregano, to taste*
Dried thyme	*A dash of lemon juice*
25 g (1 oz) vegetarian sheep's cheese	*½ small cucumber, weighing about 200 g (7 oz)*
2 stoned olives	*15 g (½ oz) butter*
½ small aubergine, weighing about 100 g (3½ oz)	*55 g (2 oz) mushrooms, about the same diameter as the cucumber*
½ small courgette, weighing about 55 g (2 oz)	*10 ml (2 tsp) fresh chopped mint or parsley*

Method

1
Hollow out each tomato and season with salt, pepper and thyme to taste.

2
Slice the sheep's cheese and fill each tomato with a small slice of cheese.

3
Slice the olives in half and close each tomato with a lid of a half olive.

4
Cut both the aubergine and courgette in half lengthways.

5
Cut both vegetables into slices about 2-cm (¾-in) thick.

6
In a bowl, season the oil with salt and pepper and stir in the oregano and lemon juice. Add the vegetables, stir to mix and leave to marinate for 10 minutes.

7
Cut the cucumber into slices about 3-cm (1¼-in) thick.

8
Hollow out and discard the centre and seeds with a small spoon and season the cucumber with salt and pepper.

9
Melt the butter in a pan and cook the mushrooms with salt and pepper to taste for 5 minutes. Sprinkle with chopped mint or parsley.

10
Stuff the cucumber slices with the mushrooms.

11
Press the tomatoes, aubergine, courgette and cucumber slices alternately onto 2 kebab skewers, then brush the kebabs with the aubergine and courgette marinade.

12
Place on a grill rack and cook under a preheated grill for about 10 minutes, turning the kebabs frequently to cook them evenly. Serve hot.

Serving suggestion
Serve with pitta bread and a red Greek wine.

Variations
Use vegetarian Cheddar or Mozzarella cheese in place of sheep's cheese. Use sesame oil in place of olive oil.

Curried Potatoes

These spicy potatoes make a satisfying snack or accompaniment.

Preparation time: 10 minutes • Cooking time: 25 minutes • Serves: 1

Ingredients

250 g (9 oz) potatoes	1-cm (¹/₂-in) piece fresh root ginger, finely chopped
Salt	1 clove garlic, crushed
30 ml (2 tbsp) vegetable oil	7.5 ml (1¹/₂ tsp) curry powder
1 onion, thinly sliced	15-30 ml (1-2 tbsp) sesame seeds

Method

1
Peel the potatoes and cut into cubes.

2
Season the potato cubes with salt, then heat the oil in a pan and cook the potatoes for 10 minutes, turning frequently to cook evenly.

3
Add the onion, ginger, garlic and curry powder to the potatoes.

4
Add about 50 ml (2 fl oz) water to the pan and stir to mix. Cover and cook for 10-12 minutes, stirring occasionally, until the potatoes are cooked and tender.

5
Taste and adjust the seasoning and serve immediately, sprinkled with sesame seeds.

Serving suggestion
Serve with a shredded vegetable salad.

Variations
Use 1 leek in place of the onion. Use sweet potatoes in place of standard potatoes. Use chilli powder in place of curry powder.

Cook's tip
Curry paste can be used in place of curry powder.

Stuffed Courgette

Creamed coconut and spices give this vegetable dish an exotic flavour.

Preparation time: 20 minutes • Cooking time: 30-45 minutes • Serves: 1

Ingredients

1 medium courgette	1.25 ml (¼ tsp) cumin seeds
10 ml (2 tsp) olive oil	A pinch of turmeric
½ small onion, very finely chopped	A pinch of asafoetida powder (optional)
25 g (1 oz) carrot, grated	25 g (1 oz) creamed coconut, grated
A pinch of paprika	Fresh herb sprigs, to garnish

Method

1
Cut the courgette in half lengthways.

2
Using a teaspoon, remove the flesh leaving about a 5-mm (¼-in) shell.

3
Finely chop the flesh and set aside.

4
Heat the oil in a pan, add the onion and cook for a few minutes, stirring occasionally, until softened.

5
Add the carrot, courgette flesh and spices and cook, stirring frequently, for a further 5 minutes, until softened.

6
Remove from the heat and stir in the creamed coconut.

7
Pile the mixture into the courgette shells, making sure that it covers the exposed part of the flesh.

8
Place the courgette halves in a greased ovenproof casserole dish and cook in a preheated oven at 190°C/375°F/Gas Mark 5 for 30-45 minutes, until the courgette shells are soft.

9
Serve immediately, garnished with fresh herb sprigs.

Serving suggestions
Serve the courgette halves on their own as a snack, or with parsley sauce and boiled new potatoes for a light lunch.

Variations
Use 1 small leek or shallot in place of onion. Use parsnip in place of carrot.

Cook's tip
Creamed coconut can be bought at delicatessens, healthfood shops and most supermarkets.
Asafoetida powder is available from Indian food shops.

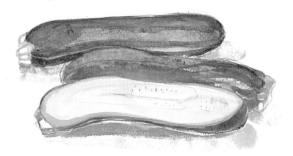

Vegetable Mini Pizzas

These flavourful vegetable snacks will make a welcome treat any time of day.

Preparation time: 20 minutes, plus kneading and rising time • Cooking time: 20 minutes • Serves: 1

Ingredients

For the dough

10 g (¼ oz) fresh yeast

150 g (5½ oz) wholemeal flour

Salt and freshly ground black pepper

Fresh basil sprigs, to garnish

For the topping

1 tomato, sliced

Chopped fresh basil

or

1 small courgette, sliced

5 ml (1 tsp) vegetable oil

1 clove garlic, crushed

Chopped fresh sage or basil

15 ml (1 tbsp) grated vegetarian hard cheese such as Cheddar or Parmesan

Method

1
For the dough, crumble the yeast into a bowl and add 15-30 ml (1-2 tbsp) lukewarm water.
Stir the mixture to ensure there are no lumps.

2
Sift the flour into a mixing bowl, make a well in the centre of the flour and add a little salt and the yeast mixture.

3
Work a little of the flour into the yeast, then cover with the remaining flour.

4
Cover with a clean cloth and leave in a warm place for about 15 minutes.

5
Add a further 100 ml (3½ fl oz) lukewarm water and knead for about 5 minutes, to form a smooth dough.

6
Cover once more and leave to rise in a warm place until the dough has doubled in size.

7
Roll out the dough until about 1-cm (½-in) thick. Cut out about 6 rounds with a pastry cutter.

8
Retain 2 rounds for immediate use and store the remainder in the freezer for future use.
Pack the pizza bases separately in freezer bags and freeze for up to 3 months.

9
For the topping, cover the pizza bases with slices of tomato and chopped basil, then season with salt and pepper.

10
Alternatively, cook the courgette slices in hot oil in a pan with the garlic for 5 minutes. Season with salt to taste.

11
Place the cooked courgette slices on the pizza bases and sprinkle with the chopped herbs and cheese.

12
Bake the mini pizzas in a preheated oven at 200°C/400°F/Gas Mark 6 for about 20 minutes, until cooked and golden brown. Serve hot or cold, garnished with fresh basil sprigs.

Serving suggestions
Serve with garlic or herb-flavoured crème fraîche or Greek yogurt.

Variations
Use white flour in place of wholemeal flour. Use fresh parsley or coriander in place of basil.
Use 4-6 mushrooms, sliced, in place of the courgette.

Mushrooms and Tofu in Garlic Butter

This inviting dish – ideal for a light lunch or supper – is quick and easy to make.

Preparation time: 10 minutes • Cooking time: 10-12 minutes • Serves: 1

Ingredients

25 g (1 oz) butter	*55 g (2 oz) button mushrooms*
1 small clove garlic, crushed	*55 g (2 oz) smoked tofu, cubed*
5-mm (¼-in) piece fresh root ginger, grated	*10 ml (2 tsp) chopped fresh parsley*

Method

1
Melt the butter in a frying pan.

2
Add the garlic and ginger and fry gently for 2 minutes, stirring occasionally.

3
Add the mushrooms and cook gently for 4-5 minutes, until the mushrooms are softened, stirring occasionally.

4
Add the smoked tofu and cook gently until hot, stirring occasionally.

5
Place on a warm plate, sprinkle with chopped parsley and serve at once.

Serving suggestions
Serve with crusty French bread or a crusty wholemeal roll.

Variations
Use asparagus tips in place of mushrooms. Use unsmoked tofu for a change. Use fresh basil or coriander in place of parsley.

Cook's tip
Ready-prepared fresh root ginger is available in jars, to save a little time.

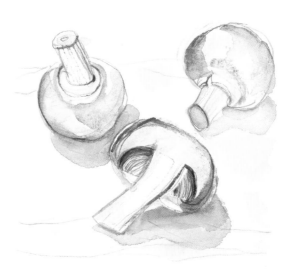

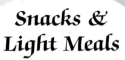

Snacks &
Light Meals

Chicory Salad with Black Grapes

This attractive salad is full of varied texture and flavour, and enhanced with a lemon yogurt dressing.

Preparation time: 15 minutes • Serves: 1

Ingredients

55 g (2 oz) plain yogurt	*1 apple, peeled, cored and sliced*
5-10 ml (1-2 tsp) lemon juice	*1 small orange, peeled and segmented*
5 ml (1 tsp) chopped lemon balm	*15 g (½ oz) sunflower seeds*
Salt	*55 g (2 oz) black grapes*
Sugar	*Lemon balm leaves, to garnish*
1 small head chicory, leaves separated	

Method

1
For the dressing, in a bowl, mix the yogurt with the lemon juice, lemon balm and salt and sugar to taste.
Stir the ingredients together to mix well, then set aside.

2
Arrange the chicory leaves, apple slices and orange segments on a serving plate.

3
Sprinkle the salad with sunflower seeds and scatter the grapes on top.

4
Garnish with lemon balm leaves and serve with the yogurt dressing spooned into the centre of the salad or alongside.

Serving suggestion
Serve with thin slices of bread and butter.

Variations
Use 1 pear in place of the apple. Use fresh parsley in place of lemon balm. Use pumpkin seeds in place of sunflower seeds.

Butter Bean, Lemon and Fennel Salad

This interesting salad makes an unusual lunch or supper dish.

Preparation time: 15 minutes, plus standing time • Cooking time: 1 hour 20 minutes (microwave) • Serves: 1

Ingredients

55 g (2 oz) dried butter beans	A pinch of sugar
½ small bulb fennel, thinly sliced (fronds reserved for the dressing)	Salt and freshly ground black pepper
	Lettuce and radicchio leaves, for serving
1 lemon	Fresh herb sprigs, to garnish
15 ml (1 tbsp) vegetable oil	

Method

1
Place the beans in a bowl and cover completely with cold water. Cook in a microwave oven on HIGH for 10 minutes, then remove and allow to stand for 1 hour.

2
Drain the beans and discard the cooking liquid. Return the beans to the bowl and cover with fresh water.

3
Cook the beans on MEDIUM for 1 hour. Leave to stand for 10 minutes before draining thoroughly.

4
Place 150 ml (¼ pint) water in a bowl and cook on HIGH for 5-7 minutes.

5
Blanch the fennel slices in the boiling water for 2 minutes on HIGH. Drain the fennel thoroughly and set aside.

6
Remove the rind from the lemon using a potato peeler. Make sure to remove any white pith from the rind.

7
Cut the rind into very thin strips and set aside for garnishing.

8
Squeeze the juice from the lemon. Place 10 ml (2 tsp) lemon juice, the oil, sugar and salt and pepper to taste in a small bowl and whisk together with a fork or small whisk until the mixture is thick.

9
Finely chop the reserved fennel fronds and add to the dressing.

10
Mix the cooked beans and fennel together in a bowl.

11
Pour over the lemon dressing and mix well to coat all the ingredients thoroughly.

12
Serve on a bed of mixed lettuce and radicchio. Garnish with fresh herb sprigs and the reserved lemon rind.

Serving suggestions
Serve with boiled new potatoes in their skins or baked potatoes.

Variations
Use other dried beans such as flageolet or black-eyed beans in place of butter beans. Use lime rind and juice in place of lemon. Use walnut or hazelnut oil for a tasty variation.

Cucumber and Pineapple Salad

This is a refreshing salad for a light, summer meal.

Preparation time: 10 minutes, plus 30 minutes soaking time • Serves: 1

Ingredients

5 ml (1 tsp) raisins	*55 g (2 oz) prepared pineapple*
15 ml (1 tbsp) pineapple juice	*15 ml (1 tbsp) French dressing*
70 g (2½ oz) cucumber	*A pinch of finely chopped fresh mint*
½ small red pepper	*A large pinch of sesame seeds*

Method

1
Soak the raisins in the pineapple juice in a bowl for at least ½ hour.

2
Thinly slice the cucumber.

3
Seed the pepper and finely chop.

4
Chop the pineapple into cubes.

5
Arrange the cucumber on a serving plate.

6
Mix the pepper, pineapple and soaked raisins together and pile into the centre of the cucumber.

7
Mix the French dressing and mint together and pour over the salad just before serving.

8
Sprinkle the sesame seeds over the top and serve immediately.

Serving suggestions
Serve with vegetable flans and vegetable roasts for a main course or with crusty bread for a light meal.

Variations
Use sultanas in place of raisins. Use orange or apple juice in place of pineapple juice.
Use sunflower seeds in place of sesame seeds.

Cook's tip
Canned pineapple (in fruit juice) can be used if fresh pineapple is not available.

Smoked Tofu Salad

A tasty main course salad – ideal served with fresh bread.

Preparation time: 15 minutes • Serves: 1

Ingredients

55 g (2 oz) broccoli florets	*15 ml (1 tbsp) canned sweetcorn kernels, drained*
25 g (1 oz) mushrooms	*15 ml (1 tbsp) French dressing*
25 g (1 oz) prepared pineapple	*55 g (2 oz) smoked tofu, cut into cubes*

Method

1
Cover the broccoli florets with boiling water in a bowl and leave to stand for 5 minutes. Drain and allow to cool.

2
Thinly slice the mushrooms.

3
Cut the pineapple into small pieces.

4
Place the broccoli, mushrooms, pineapple and sweetcorn in a bowl together with the French dressing. Mix carefully.

5
Place the salad on a serving dish and place the smoked tofu on top. Serve at once.

Serving suggestions
Serve with warmed ciabatta or pitta bread.

Variations
Omit the tofu and serve as a side salad with savoury vegetable flans. Use cauliflower florets in place of broccoli. Use mango in place of pineapple. Use canned chick-peas or kidney beans, rinsed and drained, in place of sweetcorn.

Cook's tip
If using unsmoked tofu, marinate for a few hours in equal parts of shoyu (Japanese soy sauce) and olive oil with a little crushed garlic and fresh grated ginger.

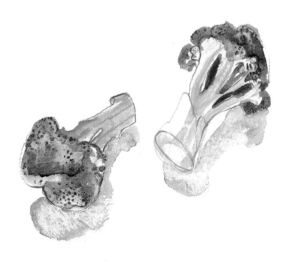

Carrot and Celery Salad

A delightfully crunchy salad with a touch of heat in the dressing.

Preparation time: 10 minutes, plus 30 minutes chilling time • Serves: 1

Ingredients

55 g (2 oz) carrots	*1.25 ml (¹/₄ tsp) paprika*
25 g (1 oz) celery	*A pinch of chilli powder*
¹/₄ red pepper	*15 ml (1 tbsp) French dressing*
25 g (1 oz) shelled walnuts	*A fresh herb sprig, to garnish*
15 ml (1 tbsp) canned sweetcorn kernels, drained	

Method

1
Scrub the carrots, then dice.

2
Thinly slice the celery.

3
Remove and discard the core and seeds from the pepper, then dice the flesh.

4
Place the carrots, celery and pepper in a serving bowl and add the walnuts and sweetcorn. Stir to mix.

5
Mix the paprika and chilli powder into the French dressing and pour over the salad.

6
Mix well and refrigerate for 30 minutes before serving. Serve, garnished with a fresh herb sprig.

Serving suggestions
Serve with quartered hard-boiled eggs for a snack, or as an accompaniment to pasta and grain dishes.

Variations
Use raw beetroot in place of carrots. Use 1 spring onion in place of celery. Use almonds or pecan nuts in place of walnuts.

Asparagus Salad

A delightful way to enjoy fresh, tender asparagus spears.

Preparation time: 20-25 minutes • Cooking time: 10-15 minutes • Serves: 1

Ingredients

	For the dressing
175 g (6 oz) asparagus	30 ml (2 tbsp) garlic oil
4 radishes	20 ml (4 tsp) herb vinegar
85 g (3 oz) cherry tomatoes	1.25 ml (¼ tsp) mild mustard
85 g (3 oz) small potatoes, cooked and peeled	Salt and freshly ground black pepper
2 spring onions	Spring onion leaves or chives, partly chopped, to garnish

Method

1

Discard any woody ends from the asparagus and peel the stems. Bring a pan of salted water to the boil, then cook the asparagus for about 10-15 minutes, until tender.

2

Remove the asparagus, drain well, then slice into pieces about 5 cm (2 in) long. Set aside.

3

Trim and slice the radishes. Remove and discard the stalks and cores from the tomatoes, then cut into slices.

4

Cut the potatoes into slices. Trim the spring onions, then cut into thin slices.

5

In a bowl, mix the asparagus, radishes, tomatoes, potatoes and spring onions together.

6

For the dressing, whisk the oil, vinegar and mustard together in a bowl and season with salt and pepper to taste.

7

Add the dressing to the vegetable salad, carefully mix together thoroughly and set aside for 30 minutes before serving, to allow the flavours to mingle.

8

Serve, garnished with the spring onion leaves or chives.

Serving suggestions

Serve with crusty French bread or a ciabatta roll.

Variations

Use baby plum tomatoes in place of cherry tomatoes. Use walnut or hazelnut oil or olive oil in place of garlic oil. Use baby sweetcorn in place of asparagus.

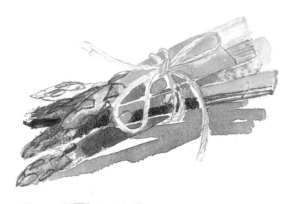

Multi-Coloured Pasta Salad

An attractive pasta salad with mixed vegetables and a mayonnaise dressing.

Preparation time: 15 minutes • Cooking time: 20 minutes • Serves: 1

Ingredients

55 g (2 oz) farfalle or pasta bows	*45-60 ml (3-4 tbsp) mayonnaise*
85 g (3 oz) carrots, sliced	*1 hard-boiled egg, quartered*
55 g (2 oz) cauliflower, broken into florets	*Fresh herb sprigs, to garnish*
55 g (2 oz) frozen peas	

Method

1
Cook the pasta in a pan of boiling water for 8-10 minutes, until just cooked or al dente.

2
Rinse, drain thoroughly and set aside to cool.

3
Meanwhile, cook the carrots in a pan of boiling water, covered, for about 5 minutes,
then add the cauliflower and cook for 4 minutes.

4
Add the peas and cook for a further 1-2 minutes, until cooked.

5
Drain the vegetables and set aside to cool.

6
Once cool, place the vegetables in a bowl with the pasta and mix well.

7
Add the mayonnaise and toss to mix, then add the hard-boiled egg quarters and carefully mix again.
Serve, garnished with fresh herb sprigs.

Serving suggestions
Serve with fresh crusty French bread or ciabatta.

Variations
Use broccoli in place of cauliflower. Use a yogurt dressing in place of mayonnaise for a reduced-fat alternative.
Use sweetcorn kernels in place of peas.

Lollo Rosso Salad

This is a colourful variation on the traditional Greek salad.

Preparation time: 10 minutes • Serves: 1

Ingredients

A few leaves of Lollo Rosso lettuce	*55 g (2 oz) vegetarian Cheshire cheese, diced or crumbled*
1 tomato, diced	*4 black olives*
¼ red pepper, seeded and chopped	
¼ green pepper, seeded and chopped	***For the dressing***
1 stick celery, sliced	*5 ml (1 tsp) tarragon vinegar*
55 g (2 oz) cucumber, diced	*15 ml (1 tbsp) olive oil*

Method

1

Break the lettuce into pieces with your fingers and place in a bowl.

2

Add the tomato, peppers, celery, cucumber and cheese and stir to mix.

3

For the dressing, mix together the vinegar and oil in a small bowl and drizzle over the salad. Toss gently to mix.

4

Place the salad on a serving dish and top with the olives. Serve.

Serving suggestion

Serve for lunch with a crusty roll or French bread.

Variations

If you do not like olives, use halved, seeded black grapes instead. Use 1 spring onion in place of celery.
Use vegetarian Cheddar cheese in place of Cheshire. Use radishes in place of cucumber.

Cook's tip

To keep celery crisp, wash well and place the sticks in a jug of cold water in the refrigerator.

Black-Eyed Beans and Orange Salad

This appetising salad has a delightfully fresh taste which is given 'bite' by the addition of watercress.

Preparation time: 20 minutes, plus standing time • Cooking time: 1 hour 10-12 minutes (microwave) • Serves: 1

Ingredients

55 g (2 oz) dried black-eyed beans	*1 spring onion, chopped*
1 bay leaf	*10 ml (2 tsp) chopped fresh parsley*
1 slice onion	*10 ml (2 tsp) chopped fresh basil leaves*
Juice and grated rind of ½ small orange	*Salt and freshly ground black pepper*
15 ml (1 tbsp) olive or grapeseed oil	*1 whole orange*
2 black olives, stoned and quartered	*Watercress, to serve*

Method

1
Place the beans in a microwave-proof bowl and cover with cold water.

2
Cook in a microwave oven on HIGH for 10-12 minutes, allow to stand for 1 hour, then drain the beans and discard the cooking liquid.

3
Return the beans to the bowl and re-cover with fresh water. Add the bay leaf and onion slice.

4
Cover the bowl with cling film and pierce several times with the tip of a sharp knife. Cook on MEDIUM for 1 hour, then stand for 10 minutes before draining thoroughly. Discard the bay leaf and onion.

5
Place the orange juice, rind and oil in a bowl and whisk with a fork.

6
Stir the olives, spring onion and chopped herbs into the orange and oil dressing.

7
Add the cooked, drained beans to the dressing mixture in the bowl, season to taste with salt and pepper and mix thoroughly to coat the beans well.

8
Carefully peel the orange, removing as much white pith as possible.

9
Cut the orange into segments, removing and discarding the thin inner membrane and any remaining white pith from each segment.

10
Reserve 1 or 2 orange segments and chop the remaining segments. Mix these chopped segments into the bean salad.

11
Arrange the watercress on a serving plate and top with the bean and orange salad.

12
Arrange the remaining orange slices on the plate for garnish and serve immediately.

Serving suggestions
Serve in split wholemeal pitta bread or in taco shells.

Variations
Use 1 stick celery in place of spring onion. Use walnut or hazelnut oil in place of olive oil. Use fresh chives in place of basil.

Savoury Bean Pot

A hearty and spicy dish for a satisfying meal for one.

Preparation time: 20 minutes • Cooking time: 30 minutes • Serves: 1

Ingredients

10 ml (2 tsp) vegetable oil	2.5 ml (½ tsp) dried mustard
½ vegetable stock cube, crumbled	A pinch of dried oregano
1 small onion, chopped	A pinch of ground cumin
1 small eating apple, peeled and grated	2.5 ml (½ tsp) brown sugar
1 small carrot, grated	Salt and freshly ground black pepper
15 ml (1 tbsp) tomato purée	115 g (4 oz) cooked red kidney beans
10 ml (2 tsp) white wine vinegar	A little soured cream

Method

1

Heat the oil in a non-stick pan. Add the crumbled stock cube, onion, apple and carrot.

2

Cook gently for 5 minutes, stirring continuously.

3

In a bowl, mix the tomato purée with 75 ml (5 tbsp) water and add to the pan together with all the other ingredients, except the beans and cream.

4

Stir well, cover and simmer for 2 minutes.

5

Add the beans, stir to mix, then transfer the mixture to an ovenproof casserole dish.

6

Cover and cook at 180°C/350°F/Gas Mark 4 for about 30 minutes.

7

Add a little more water after 20 minutes, if necessary.

8

Top with a swirl of soured cream and serve immediately.

Serving suggestions

Serve with a mixed salad and crusty fresh bread, boiled rice or a baked potato.

Variations

Use cider vinegar in place of white wine vinegar. Use 1 leek in place of the onion. Use other cooked beans such as flageolet or black-eyed beans in place of kidney beans.

Cook's tip

Canned kidney beans are ideal for this recipe and save you having to cook the beans yourself at home.

Tortellini with Vegetables

Tender tortellini are tossed with a blue cheese and vegetable sauce to create this delectable dish.

Preparation time: 10 minutes • Cooking time: 15-20 minutes • Serves: 1

Ingredients

115 g (4 oz) dried vegetarian tortellini, such as mixed cheese or spinach and ricotta	*85 g (3 oz) mangetout, trimmed*
15 g (½ oz) butter	*3 cherry tomatoes*
2 spring onions, chopped	*Salt and freshly ground black pepper*
45 ml (3 tbsp) double cream	*1 sage leaf, finely chopped*
25 g (1 oz) vegetarian Gorgonzola	*1 shelled chopped walnut, to garnish*

Method

1
Cook the tortellini in a large saucepan of lightly salted, boiling water until just cooked or al dente.

2
Drain well, set aside and keep hot.

3
Melt the butter in a pan, add the spring onions and cook for 5 minutes, until softened, stirring occasionally.

4
Pour the cream into the pan, then crumble the Gorgonzola and add to the pan, heating gently until the cheese has melted, stirring.

5
Add the mangetout to the sauce and allow to cook for about 1 minute, stirring occasionally.

6
Remove the stalks and cores from the tomatoes, add to the sauce and season with salt and pepper.

7
Add the chopped sage leaf to the sauce and stir to mix.

8
Add the cooked tortellini to the sauce and stir to mix.

9
Reheat gently until hot, then serve immediately, garnished with chopped walnut.

Serving suggestion
Serve with crusty French bread and a mixed leaf salad.

Variations
Use vegetarian Stilton in place of Gorgonzola. Use sugar snap peas or sliced mushrooms in place of mangetout. Use crème fraîche in place of cream.

Moors and Christians

This dish, originally from Cuba, is so called because of the use of black beans and white rice.

Preparation time: 10 minutes • Cooking time: 1-1½ hours for the beans; 25-30 minutes for the finished dish • Serves: 1

Ingredients

55 g (2 oz) black beans, soaked overnight and cooked until soft	*½ small green pepper, seeded and finely chopped*
10 ml (2 tsp) vegetable oil	*1 tomato, skinned and finely chopped*
½ small onion, chopped	*70 g (2½ oz) long-grain rice*
1 clove garlic, crushed	*Salt and freshly ground black pepper*
	A fresh herb sprig, to garnish

Method

1

Drain the cooked beans and mash 15 ml (1 tbsp) to a paste with a fork, adding a little water if necessary. Set aside.

2

Heat the oil in a pan and fry the onion, garlic and pepper until soft, stirring occasionally.

3

Add the tomato and cook for a further 2 minutes.

4

Add the bean paste and stir to mix.

5

Add the cooked beans and rice, and enough water to cover.

6

Bring to the boil, cover and simmer for 20-25 minutes, until the rice is just cooked or al dente, stirring occasionally.

7

Season to taste with salt and pepper, and serve hot, garnished with a fresh herb sprig.

Serving suggestion

Serve with a crisp green salad and crusty bread.

Variations

Use other beans such as flageolet or butter beans in place of black beans. Use 1 baby leek in place of onion.

Mushroom Stroganoff

This creamy, herb-flavoured mushroom dish is sure to become a real favourite.

Preparation time: 10 minutes • Cooking time: 20 minutes • Serves: 1

Ingredients

1 small onion, sliced	*5 ml (1 tsp) unbleached flour*
1 stick celery, chopped	*75 ml (5 tbsp) vegetable stock*
15 g (½ oz) butter	*Salt and freshly ground black pepper*
115 g (4 oz) tiny button mushrooms	*15 ml (1 tbsp) soured cream or yogurt*
A pinch of dried mixed herbs	*Chopped fresh parsley, to garnish*
A pinch of dried basil	

Method

1

Place the onion and celery in a pan together with the butter and cook over a low heat until the onions are transparent, stirring occasionally.

2

Add the mushrooms and cook for 2-3 minutes, until the juices run, stirring occasionally.

3

Add the mixed herbs and basil.

4

Stir in the flour and cook gently for 1 minute, stirring.

5

Stir in the stock and seasoning and cook gently for 8-10 minutes, stirring occasionally.

6

Remove from the heat, stir in the soured cream or yogurt and adjust the seasoning if necessary.

7

Heat very gently until hot but do not allow to boil.

8

Garnish with the chopped parsley and serve at once.

Serving suggestion

Serve on a bed of walnut rice – cook enough rice to serve 1 person, then carefully fold in salt and pepper to taste, a little butter, a little crushed garlic and 15 g (½ oz) finely chopped walnuts.

Variations

Use 1 small leek or 2 shallots in place of the onion. Use crème fraîche in place of soured cream.

Cook's tip

If tiny button mushrooms are not available, use the larger variety and thickly slice.

Main Dishes

Chana Masala

An excellent dish to serve hot as a main course, or cold as an accompaniment to a nut loaf.

Preparation time: 15 minutes • Cooking time: 30 minutes • Serves: 1

Ingredients

½ small onion, chopped	2.5 ml (½ tsp) roasted cumin seeds, ground
1 clove garlic, crushed	5 ml (1 tsp) dried mango powder (amchur) or lemon juice
5-mm (¼-in) piece fresh root ginger, finely chopped	2.5 ml (½ tsp) paprika
15 ml (1 tbsp) clarified butter or ghee	100 g (3½ oz) canned tomatoes
5 ml (1 tsp) ground coriander	175 g (6 oz) cooked chick-peas
2.5 ml (½ tsp) cumin seeds	1.25 ml (¼ tsp) garam masala
A pinch of cayenne pepper	Salt, to taste
1.25 ml (¼ tsp) turmeric	½ small fresh green chilli, finely chopped

Method

1

Cook the onion, garlic and ginger in the clarified butter or ghee in a pan until softened, stirring occasionally.

2

Add all the spices, except the garam masala, and cook over a low heat for 1-2 minutes, stirring continuously.

3

Add the tomatoes, roughly chopped, together with their juice.

4

Add the cooked chick-peas and mix well.

5

Cook for 30 minutes over a medium heat, stirring occasionally.

6

Add the garam masala, salt and chilli, stir well and serve immediately.

Serving suggestions

Serve hot with boiled or pilau rice and mango chutney. This dish improves with time and is always more flavourful the following day.

Variations

Small pieces of diced vegetables such as potatoes, fresh tomatoes or cauliflower can be added to the dish at the start of cooking. Use cooked kidney or flageolet beans in place of chick-peas.

Cook's tip

Fry the spices over a low heat to ensure that they do not burn.

66

Tabouleh

This traditional Middle-Eastern dish is delicious yet quick and easy to make.

Preparation time: 15 minutes, plus standing time • Serves: 1

Ingredients

30 ml (2 tbsp) cooked, prepared couscous	*Juice of ½ lemon*
1 large tomato, finely chopped	*Finely grated rind of 1 lemon*
125 g (4½ oz) cucumber, finely chopped	*5 ml (1 tsp) finely chopped fresh flat-leafed parsley*
1 shallot, thinly sliced	*5 ml (1 tsp) finely chopped fresh mint*
Salt and freshly ground black pepper	*A lemon slice and fresh herb sprig, to garnish*

Method

1

Rinse the couscous under running cold water in a very fine sieve. Place in a bowl.

2

Add the tomato, cucumber, shallot, salt and pepper to taste, lemon juice and lemon rind.

3

Stir the mixture together well, cover and set aside in a cool place for half a day.

4

Add the chopped herbs to the couscous mixture, taste and adjust the seasoning.

5

Serve, garnished with the lemon slice and fresh herb sprig.

Serving suggestion

Serve on a bed of lettuce with a poached egg on top.

Variations

Use cooked, prepared bulgur wheat in place of couscous. Use lime juice and rind in place of lemon.
Use mushrooms or radishes in place of cucumber.

Quick Vegetable Chilli

This popular, spicy dish is always a tasty treat.

Preparation time: 10 minutes • Cooking time: 25-30 minutes • Serves: 1

Ingredients

1 onion, sliced	55 g (2 oz) cauliflower florets
5 ml (1 tsp) olive oil	1 small carrot, roughly chopped
¼ clove garlic, crushed	2.5 ml (½ tsp) tomato purée
1.25 ml (¼ tsp) chilli powder	A pinch of dried basil
100 g (3½ oz) canned tomatoes, chopped	A pinch of dried oregano
100 g (3½ oz) cooked red kidney beans	75 ml (5 tbsp) vegetable stock
¼ small red pepper, seeded and roughly chopped	A fresh herb sprig, to garnish
¼ medium courgette, sliced into chunks	

Method

1
Cook the onion in the oil in a pan until softened, stirring occasionally.

2
Add the garlic and cook gently for 1 minute, stirring.

3
Add the chilli powder and cook gently for a further minute, stirring.

4
Add the remaining ingredients, except the garnish, mix well and simmer for 25-30 minutes, stirring occasionally.

5
Serve immediately, garnished with a fresh herb sprig.

Serving suggestions
Serve with boiled brown or white rice, couscous or bulgur wheat.

Variations
Use broccoli in place of cauliflower, or sliced mushrooms. Use 1 leek in place of the onion.

Sweet Bean Curry

This bean curry is sweetened with apple and sultanas, and enriched with creamed coconut.

Preparation time: 1 hour 20 minutes • Cooking time: 25-30 minutes • Serves: 1

Ingredients

40 g (1½ oz) red kidney beans, soaked overnight	150 ml (¼ pint) bean stock or bean stock and water
A knob of butter	Salt and freshly ground black pepper
½ small onion, sliced	5 ml (1 tsp) lemon juice
½ small apple, cored and chopped	5 ml (1 tsp) chutney
40 g (1½ oz) mushrooms, sliced	15 g (½ oz) sultanas
5 ml (1 tsp) curry powder	15 g (½ oz) creamed coconut, grated or chopped
10 g (¼ oz) unbleached flour	A fresh herb sprig and quarters of hard-boiled egg, to garnish

Method

1
Drain the beans, place in a pan and cover with cold water.

2
Bring to the boil and boil vigorously for 10-15 minutes, then lower the heat and boil for about 1 hour, until the beans are tender but still whole. Drain and set aside.

3
Melt the butter in a pan and cook the onion until very brown, stirring occasionally.

4
Add the apple and mushrooms and cook for 2-3 minutes, stirring occasionally.

5
Add the curry powder and flour and cook for 1-2 minutes, stirring continuously.

6
Gradually add the bean stock or bean stock and water and stir until smooth.

7
Add the seasoning, lemon juice, chutney, sultanas and cooked beans and simmer for 10-15 minutes, stirring occasionally.

8
Just before serving, add the creamed coconut and stir until dissolved.

9
Serve hot, garnished with a fresh herb sprig and egg quarters.

Serving suggestion
Serve with boiled brown rice and fried plantains – peel, cut into 1-cm (½-in) slices and fry in hot oil until golden brown. If unavailable, use unripe green bananas.

Variations
Use chick-peas in place of kidney beans. Use chilli powder in place of curry powder. Use ½ pear in place of apple.

Courgettes Mediterranean-Style

The addition of haricot beans makes this vegetable dish a filling main course served with rice.

Preparation time: 10 minutes • Cooking time: 35 minutes • Serves: 1

Ingredients

15 ml (1 tbsp) olive oil	*100 g (3½ oz) canned tomatoes*
1 small onion, finely chopped	*115 g (4 oz) courgettes, thinly sliced*
1 clove garlic, crushed	*1.25 ml (¼ tsp) dried oregano*
½ red pepper, seeded and chopped	*Salt and freshly ground black pepper*
55 g (2 oz) cooked haricot beans	

Method

1
Heat the oil in a pan.

2
Add the onion, garlic and pepper and cook for 4-5 minutes, stirring occasionally.

3
Add the cooked beans, tomatoes and courgettes and stir well.

4
Add the oregano and salt and pepper to taste, then stir again.

5
Cover and cook slowly for 30 minutes, stirring occasionally.

6
Adjust the seasoning and serve.

Serving suggestions
Serve on a bed of boiled white, brown or wild rice.

Variations
Use cooked flageolet or butter beans in place of haricot beans. Use sliced mushrooms in place of courgettes. Use dried mixed herbs in place of oregano.

Cook's tip
This dish will reheat well. Always reheat thoroughly until piping hot.

Penne with Roquefort Cream Sauce

Pasta tubes are tossed with a creamy cheese and mushroom sauce.

Preparation time: 10 minutes • Cooking time: 15-20 minutes • Serves: 1

Ingredients

55 g (2 oz) vegetarian Roquefort cheese	*15 g (1/2 oz) butter*
125 ml (4 fl oz) double cream	*55 g (2 oz) mushrooms, thinly sliced*
Salt and freshly ground black pepper	*100 g (3 1/2 oz) dried tricolour penne*

Method

1

Crumble the Roquefort cheese and add to the cream in a pan. Mix well.

2

Bring the cream mixture gently to the boil, stirring, and add salt and pepper to taste.

3

Cook gently, stirring, until a creamy sauce has formed. Set aside and keep warm.

4

Melt the butter in a pan, add the mushrooms and cook for about 5 minutes, stirring occasionally, until just cooked.

5

Add salt and pepper to taste, set aside and keep warm.

6

Meanwhile, cook the pasta in a saucepan of boiling salted water for 8-10 minutes, until just cooked or al dente.

7

Drain the pasta thoroughly and return to the pan.

8

Add the mushrooms and cream sauce and toss together to mix well. Serve hot.

Serving suggestion

Serve with crusty fresh bread and a mixed pepper and tomato salad.

Variations

Use Stilton in place of Roquefort. Use crème fraîche in place of cream. Use courgettes in place of mushrooms.

Strawberry and Banana Frost

This speedy dessert can be started ahead of time and completed just before serving.

Preparation time: 10 minutes, plus freezing time • Serves: 1

Ingredients

115 g (4 oz) strawberries	*A few drops of vanilla essence*
1 small banana	*1.25 ml (¼ tsp) clear honey*
45 ml (3 tbsp) plain fromage frais	*Fresh strawberry leaves, to decorate*

Method

1

Hull the strawberries and place half in a dish in the refrigerator.

2

Peel the banana and cut into pieces.

3

Cut the remaining strawberries in half or into quarters if they are large and freeze with the banana in a container until solid.

4

Just before serving, remove the strawberries and banana from the freezer.

5

Place the frozen strawberries and banana, fromage frais, vanilla essence and honey in a food processor or blender and process until smooth. You will need to push the mixture down two or three times with a spatula or wooden spoon.

6

Place the mixture in a serving dish and arrange the remaining strawberries around the top of the frost mixture.

7

Serve at once, decorated with fresh strawberry leaves.

Serving suggestions

Serve with wafers or chocolate finger biscuits.

Variations

Use pineapple, raspberries or apple in place of strawberries. Use prepared mango in place of banana. Use almond essence in place of vanilla essence.

Cook's tip

For a creamier frost, use Greek yogurt in place of fromage frais, but this will add a few extra calories.

Orange Slices with Almonds

This quick and easy fruit dessert is refreshing and delicious.

Preparation time: 10 minutes • Cooking time: 10 minutes • Serves: 1

Ingredients

1 small orange	20 g (³/₄ oz) ground almonds
1 large orange	30 ml (2 tbsp) Grand Marnier
15 ml (1 tbsp) butter	7.5 ml (1½ tsp) lemon juice
10 ml (2 tsp) sugar	

Method

1
Thinly peel the small orange, then cut the peel into thin strips. Cut the orange flesh in half, then squeeze to collect the juice. Set aside.

2
Peel the large orange, remove any pith from the orange flesh, then thinly slice the orange.

3
Melt the butter in a shallow pan and add the sugar and ground almonds.

4
Stir and cook gently until lightly caramelised.

5
Add the orange slices and orange peel and cook the orange slices for 3 minutes on each side.

6
Flambé the oranges with Grand Marnier.

7
Stir the reserved orange juice and lemon juice into the hot pan, and serve immediately.

Serving suggestions
Serve with whipped cream or vanilla ice cream.

Variations
Use pink or red grapefruit in place of oranges. Use ground hazelnuts in place of almonds. Use lime juice in place of lemon juice.

Meringue-Topped Fruit

A simple dish of mixed stewed fruit is enhanced by a light meringue topping.

Preparation time: 10 minutes • Cooking time: 5 minutes • Serves: 1

Ingredients

250 g (9 oz) mixed stewed fruit, such as apricots and cherries	*5 ml (1 tsp) lemon juice*
1 medium egg white	*40 g (1½ oz) caster sugar*

Method

1
Place the cooled stewed fruit in an ovenproof dish.

2
Whisk the egg white with the lemon juice in a bowl until stiff.

3
Gradually whisk in the sugar.

4
Spread the meringue mixture evenly over the fruit.

5
Cook under a preheated grill for about 5 minutes, until the meringue is golden brown. Serve immediately.

Serving suggestions
Serve with a dollop of cream or crème fraîche or sponge finger biscuits.

Variations
You can add 15 ml (1 tbsp) ground almonds or other nuts to the meringue mixture. For a special treat, add a little Grand Marnier or Cointreau to the meringue mixture.

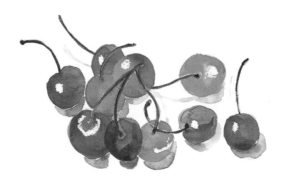

Desserts

Coffee and Raisin Ice Cream

This sumptuous ice cream makes the perfect finale to any meal, or enjoy as a treat at any time.

Preparation time: 10 minutes, plus cooling and freezing time • Cooking time: 5 minutes • Serves: 1

Ingredients

75 ml (5 tbsp) full-cream milk	1.25 ml (¼ tsp) vanilla essence
25 g (1 oz) sugar	75 ml (5 tbsp) whipping or double cream
7.5 ml (1½ tbsp) coffee granules or powder	15 g (½ oz) raisins
1.25 ml (¼ tsp) cocoa powder	Chopped nuts, to decorate
1 small egg yolk	

Method

1
Heat the milk and sugar in a pan until almost boiling.

2
Add the coffee and cocoa, stir well, then remove from the heat and set aside to cool.

3
In a small bowl, beat the egg yolk with the vanilla essence until frothy.

4
In a separate bowl, whip the cream until stiff.

5
Spoon the cream and cooled coffee mixture into the egg mixture and stir well to mix.

6
Add the raisins and mix well.

7
Freeze in a small container until firm, stirring several times during freezing.

8
Defrost for 10-15 minutes before serving. Serve, decorated with chopped nuts.

Serving suggestion
Serve with homemade cookies.

Variations
For a chocolate flavour, use light carob powder in place of coffee. Use chopped ready-to-eat dried apricots in place of raisins.

Cook's tip
Increase the ingredient quantities by 4 and keep the ice cream in the freezer for up to 1 month.

Blueberry Pancake

Pancakes are always a joy to eat, and this blueberry version is particularly delicious.

Preparation time: 10 minutes, plus 10 minutes standing time • Cooking time: 8-10 minutes • Serves: 1

Ingredients

22.5 ml (1½ tbsp) plain flour	*20 g (¾ oz) butter*
60 ml (4 tbsp) milk	*45-60 ml (3-4 tbsp) blueberries*
A pinch of salt	*Sugar, to taste*
1 medium egg	*A fresh mint sprig, to decorate*
A pinch of baking powder	

Method

1

In a bowl, beat the flour, milk and salt together with a whisk until smooth.

2

Leave the mixture to stand for about 10 minutes, then beat the egg and baking powder into the batter, mixing well.

3

Melt half the butter in a small frying or omelette pan, then pour in the batter, covering the base of the pan completely. Spread the blueberries evenly over the mixture.

4

Cook for about 4 minutes, then slide the pancake out onto a large plate to turn it.

5

Add the remaining butter to the pan and heat until melted.

6

Return the pancake to the pan, with the uncooked side of the pancake face down in the pan, and cook for a further 4-5 minutes until brown.

7

Serve the pancake on a warm plate, sprinkled with sugar. Decorate with a fresh mint sprig.

Serving suggestions

Serve with a dollop of whipped cream or a scoop of ice cream.

Variations

Use raspberries or blackberries in place of blueberries. Use wholemeal flour in place of white flour.

Desserts

Minted Grapes

This is a refreshing dessert to enjoy after a large meal.

Preparation time: 10 minutes • Serves: 1

Ingredients

70 g (2½ oz) green grapes	*Soft brown sugar, to sprinkle*
A little Crème de Menthe	*A fresh mint sprig, to decorate*
30 ml (2 tbsp) soured cream	

Method

1
Halve and seed the grapes.

2
Place the grapes in a serving glass.

3
Sprinkle with a little Crème de Menthe.

4
Top with the soured cream.

5
Sprinkle a little brown sugar over the top and serve at once, decorated with a fresh mint sprig.

Serving suggestions
Serve with sponge fingers or chocolate wafer biscuits.

Variations
Use sherry in place of the Crème de Menthe. Use yogurt in place of soured cream. Use red or black grapes in place of green grapes. Drizzle a little honey over the top in place of sugar.

Melon with Caramelised Orange Peel

This fruity dessert is laced with wine and Cointreau and sweetened with honey.

Preparation time: 20 minutes • Cooking time: 10 minutes • Serves: 1

Ingredients

1 galia or cantaloupe melon	*15 ml (1 tbsp) Cointreau*
1 orange	*1 medium egg white*
50 ml (2 fl oz) white wine	*15 ml (1 tbsp) icing sugar, sifted*
15 ml (1 tbsp) honey	

Method

1
Cut the melon in half, remove and discard the seeds, then remove the flesh from one half of the melon using a melon baller. Place the melon balls in a bowl.

2
Place the remaining melon half in the refrigerator.

3
Peel the orange very thinly, then thinly slice the peel into strips.

4
Mix the wine and honey in a pan, add the orange peel and cook until all the liquid is evaporated and the peel is caramelised, stirring frequently. Remove from the heat and set aside.

5
Remove all the pith from the peeled orange and divide into segments.

6
Chop the orange segments, then mix with the caramelised orange peel and melon balls.

7
Dissolve the remaining caramel in the pan with the Cointreau.

8
Pile the mixed fruit into the chilled melon half and return to the refrigerator to chill for 1 hour.

9
In a bowl, whisk the egg white and icing sugar together until stiff.

10
Place the mixture in an icing bag fitted with a star nozzle and pipe rosettes on top of the chilled melon so that all the fruit is covered.

11
Place under a preheated grill and cook for about 3 minutes until the meringue mixture is lightly browned. Serve immediately.

Serving suggestion
Serve with fresh whipped cream or crème fraîche.

Variations
Use 1 small red grapefruit in place of the orange. Use rosé wine in place of white wine.

Cranberry Fool

An inviting dessert – light, creamy and fruity.

Preparation time: 10 minutes • Cooking time: 10-15 minutes • Serves: 1

Ingredients

55 g (2 oz) fresh cranberries	*25 g (1 oz) Greek yogurt*
10 ml (2 tsp) clear honey	*Toasted almond flakes, to decorate*
30 ml (2 tbsp) whipping cream	

Method

1
Rinse the cranberries and gently cook in a pan with a scant amount of water until softened.

2
Remove from the heat, stir in the honey, then set aside to cool.

3
Whip the cream in a small bowl until stiff. Gently fold the yogurt into the cream.

4
Combine the yogurt and cream mixture with the cooled cranberries, folding gently to mix.

5
Place the mixture in a serving glass and decorate with the toasted almond flakes. Serve immediately.

Serving suggestion
Serve with homemade biscuits or cookies.

Variations
Use crème fraîche in place of Greek yogurt. Use chopped hazelnuts in place of almonds.

Cook's tip
Fresh cranberries are often only available at Christmas time. Redcurrants make an excellent summer substitute.

Grilled Banana

This luxurious, rich dessert is made in minutes.

Preparation time: 10 minutes • Cooking time: 4-5 minutes • Serves: 1

Ingredients

1 banana	*15 ml (1 tbsp) Mascarpone cheese or double cream*
5 ml (1 tsp) lemon juice	*15 ml (1 tbsp) milk*
10 g (¼ oz) butter	*Vanilla sugar, to taste*
A pinch of ground cinnamon	*Cranberries and a fresh herb sprig, to decorate*
5 ml (1 tsp) icing sugar or runny honey	

Method

1
Peel the banana and cut in half lengthways. Immediately sprinkle with lemon juice to prevent browning.

2
Place the banana in an ovenproof dish.

3
Melt the butter in a frying pan, then stir in the cinnamon and icing sugar or honey. Mix well and remove from the heat.

4
Coat the banana slices all over with the cinnamon mixture.

5
Place the banana slices under a preheated grill and grill for 4-5 minutes until golden brown, turning once.

6
Meanwhile, for the cream sauce, mix the Mascarpone cheese or cream together with the milk in a bowl. Add vanilla sugar to taste.

7
Serve the grilled banana with the cream sauce poured over or alongside.

8
Decorate with cranberries and the fresh herb sprig.

Serving suggestions
Serve with wafers or sponge finger biscuits.

Variations
Use ginger or mixed spice in place of cinnamon. Use crème fraîche in place of Mascarpone cheese or double cream.

Cook's tip
For a special treat, gently heat a little pear liqueur or rum, pour over the banana slices and set alight.

Index